Lakewold

A Magnificent Northwest Garden

To Janet
Where the blue poppy grows

Judy and Cordy

Foreword by Dan Hinkley

Ronald Fields, editor
Judy Wagner, producer

Dedicated to Eulalie and G. Corydon Wagner

Contents

PREFACE AND ACKNOWLEDGMENTS
Ronald Fields

The floral garden is perhaps the most malleable part of our natural environment. While it may well serve a narcissistic need to arrange, control, and manipulate, it is also enormously gratifying when it serves our aesthetic and spiritual needs. I have always dabbled in gardening projects but did not become a self-conscious gardener until twenty years ago when I discovered Lakewold Gardens. This was eye-opening, serious gardening. Yet, although Lakewold has welcomed the public since 1989, it was not designed as a public garden. On the contrary: it is a quintessentially personal garden whose many intimate elements bear the stamp of individual choice as well as horticultural connoisseurship.

Having been a docent in these gardens for twenty years, I've learned much from them and from the small library they have inspired me to acquire.

As a garden enthusiast, I relish the fact that an interest in gardening has become something of a national pastime. Garden centers and catalog companies abound, and plants that were difficult to find two decades ago are now readily available, along with all the new varieties and hybrids that are constantly being introduced. Moreover, serious gardeners can now find nearly infinite sources for plant material on the web. The temptation to collect is infectious, and restraint is the gift of a wise gardener who understands the elements of design in space and who is able to exercise aesthetic taste in spatial constructions. Effects of this kind are attainable in smaller gardens, of course; but larger and more complex gardens, such as Lakewold's, provide impressive compositions with luxuriant visual and, often, olfactory delights—plus surprising "aah" experiences that soothe (the sounds of water), amuse (tiny alpines), or charm us by the sheer abundance of it all.

These gardens are well-known. In the last four decades, Lakewold has been featured in numerous magazine and newspaper articles, and many references to it have appeared in a variety of landscape and garden books. Yet until now there has been no individual work devoted exclusively to them. This book aims to address that deficiency in a variety of ways and with a variety of voices. Following a warm and thoughtful presentation of the seasons at Lakewold in Valerie Easton's Introduction, there is, first and foremost, the extraordinary collaboration of Mrs. Corydon Wagner and the landscape architect, Mr. Thomas Church, which I have undertaken to describe in a brief historical overview of the property in chapter 1. In chapter 2, you will gain insights into Mrs. Wagner's distinctive persona through her friend and fellow garden enthusiast, Steve Lorton, while chapter 3 is devoted to Professor Marc Treib's helpful and concise introduction to the work of Thomas Church and his designs for Lakewold. Secondly, you will find more detailed reports on specific areas of interest, beginning with Garden Manager Katie Burki's discussion of some of the rare plants in the gardens, while Vickie Haushild, Proprietor of the Garden Shop, opens a window on features of the garden visitors seek out and treasure; and Bill Noble, of the Garden Conservancy of America, presents his analysis of the important issue of garden preservation.

The use of the terms "concise," "brief," and "some" in describing the written texts is deliberate. From the outset, the book was intended to be lavishly illustrated and to present the gardens not as a fixed entity but as a development in and through time. You will see vintage images and many professional photographs from the past four decades, as well as photographs by and from staff and volunteers. The generous array of illustrations is intended to encompass and document the gardens—not simply as a living legacy, but to serve as an ongoing inspiration to fellow gardeners who may, as I did, find useful ideas and the encouragement to refine their own garden efforts.

Many thanks to our accomplished contributors: Valerie Easton, garden writer for the *Pacific Northwest Magazine* of the *Seattle Times*, and who actively contributes articles to a variety of publications, including *Garden Design*. Steve Lorton, prolific writer and lecturer; now retired, he was for many years Northwest Editor and Northwest Bureau Chief for *Sunset* magazine. Marc Treib, Professor Emeritus, Department of Architecture, University of California, Berkeley, and author of numerous publications on landscape architecture, including *Thomas Church, Landscape Architect: Designing a Modern California Landscape*. Katie Burki, horticulturist, Garden Manager of Lakewold Gardens. Vickie Haushild, garden writer, Proprietor of the Lakewold Garden Shop. Bill Noble, Director of Preservation for the Garden Conservancy of America, a nonprofit organization dedicated to preserving exceptional gardens and landscapes. And a special thanks to Dan Hinkley, noted plantsman, author, lecturer, horticulturist, nurseryman, and adventurer, for being so generous in providing a Foreword for this portable visit to Lakewold Gardens.

Finally, we are all enormously grateful for the vision and support of Mr. and Mrs. Corydon Wagner III. Cordy and Judy have been engaged in every step of this publication and their marvelous guidance has been an inspiration.

FOREWORD
Dan Hinkley

Nearly three decades ago, as I emerged freshly polished from graduate school at the University of Washington, I was employed at the Bloedel Reserve on Bainbridge Island. It was during that time that I became acquainted with the owners, Prentice and Virginia Bloedel, who were still spending the summers at their beloved country estate. While they were savoring their vacation during my first year of employment, Mrs. Bloedel suggested I visit her sister, Eulalie Wagner, in her garden on Gravelly Lake to see my first Meconopsis in flower. Thus began my introduction to Lakewold Gardens.

Yet my entreé to the ambrosial climate of the Pacific Northwest began the year I moved to Seattle for my continuing education. Horticulturally focused, I lived for the duration in the endearing Stone Cottage in Washington Park Arboretum. It took little time to comprehend the staggering possibilities concerning plants that could be successfully grown in the greater Puget Sound basin.

As a keen apprentice to gardening newly arrived from the hypothermic climate of the northern Midwest, I found the notion that I might come upon a plant in its floral zenith or possessing transportative foliar effects at any month of the calendar intoxicating. Surrounding the cottage, itself in one of the best collections of woody plants in North America, were hardy palms and winter-flowering camellias, fire trees from Chile and dove trees from China. My appetite to learn, as well as possess, was ravenous. When I left the university with my degree in 1985, I was armed with a lofty plentitude of Latin binomials and an

Outside its native habitat, the perennial Himalayan blue poppy, *Meconopsis grandis*, grows well in the British Isles, and in southern Alaska down to the Puget Sound basin; farther south and the weather becomes too warm for it to succeed. Even here it is a challenge. Mrs. Wagner was nevertheless so successful that the gardens became known as *Lakewold, Where the Blue Poppy Grows*, the title of a 1987 video, expanded and reissued in 2010 as a CD documentary on the gardens. In it, the poppy is identified as *Meconopsis baileyi*. Over the last few decades, however, hybridization has generated such confusion about the identities of the species *baileyi, betonicifolia, grandis*, and *sheldonii* that The Meconopsis Group was formed in 1998 to clarify the nomenclature of these blue poppies (see meconopsis. org). At Lakewold Gardens, *Meconopsis grandis* has been the official identification of the blue poppy since the 1980s, and this is the name used to identify it throughout this book.

ABOVE: Known for its black stipes, or stems, the native Western maidenhair fern, *Adiantum aleuticum*, gracefully creates a rounded fan of hand-shaped, waving pinnae or fronds that find the mix of shade and sun at Lakewold very comfortable. The plant also has the common name of Five-fingered maidenhair fern.

ABOVE RIGHT: Some nine hundred rhododendrons and azaleas can be found in the gardens. The Northwest climate is ideal for these members of the Ericaceae family. Mrs. Wagner pursued a special interest in these plants and was an active member of the Rhododendron Species Foundation, the only institution of its kind devoted to the research and propagation of a singular cultivar.

incalculable number of trees, shrubs, and vines growing in four-inch pots—and, as an unfortunate aside, virtually no idea how to gather them together to make a garden.

As an unexpected consequence, it was my exposure early on as a Pacific Northwest horticulturist to those who could assimilate artfully the plants they so passionately collected that forever changed my vision of what a garden in its truest sense could be. It was during that first visit to Lakewold that I encountered a superb collection of plants—both woody and herbaceous—that seemed immediately less a chaotic library and more a contemplative ordering and celebration of diversity.

Although I was still well away from my own attempt at making a garden, the seeds were sown on that day for what I hoped to ultimately achieve when I had my chance. Yet it is unlikely that I could possibly have articulated that thought on that day, nor is it likely I would even have attempted to.

As youth are known for doing too well, I did not fully acknowledge those who had been and were still in the process of changing the horticultural fabric of where I now garden. They had been acquiring, evaluating, and extolling or lamenting the virtues of plants appropriate for our region long before my very own germination.

Mrs. G. Corydon Wagner II (1904–1991) gave her home and garden to the Friends of Lakewold in 1989. She remained in residence until her death two years later, enjoyed seeing the docented tours, and sometimes inconspicuously tagged along. She presented each member of the first team of docents with a gift packet of seeds for the rare *Meconopsis grandis*, the blue poppy seen at the left. The package bore the caveat, "For experienced gardeners only."

It was the solid foundation that Eulalie Wagner, along with numerous of her contemporaries, had built that expanded our collective horizons. The curse of the passionate gardener's garden is that its framework loses its novelty as it matures. Not acknowledged in this anathema is the fact that the novelty has worn thin on the plants they chose to have grown because they have been mainstreamed in commerce; they are now commonplace because they were ultimately deemed good plants deserving wider recognition in regional landscapes.

Though I am not yet as mature as Mrs. Wagner was on that day we first met in the mid-1980s to admire her blue poppies, I am sufficiently enough hardened off to now recognize that her lasting legacy was not necessarily the elevating of our adventurous spirits and her demands that we take a few risks in our plantings. Today both her generosity and that of her family ensure that Lakewold can continue to invite, instruct, and inspire for generations to come. It is a garden that I look forward to returning to on a regular basis—to admire and to watch the collection mature, evolve, and transmute as all good gardens should. And to once again acknowledge a garden whose aesthetic impact on my eventual garden will echo throughout the decades ahead.

1. Entrance
2. Parking
3. Circle Drive
4. Tom Gillies Hardy Fern Garden
5. Parterres
6. Brick Walk
7. Swimming Pool and Lion Fountain
8. Helen Weyerhaeuser Tea House (Gazebo)
9. Wolf Tree and Shade Garden
10. Garden of Peace
11. Ponds and Woodland Garden
12. Picnic Point
13. Rock Garden
14. Rose and Cutting Garden
15. Knot Garden
16. The Wagner House
17. Garden Shop

LAKEWOLD GARDENS TIMELINE

15,000 years ago | Vashon Glacier recedes to reveal present-day Puget Sound and the Columbia Basin region. Lakewold exists on what is called a gravelly outwash plain. These same glacier-rounded rocks will be used later to construct the rustic rock pillars of Lakewold's perimeter fence.

1833 | Hudson's Bay Company establishes a fur-trading post at Fort Nisqually. Property that included Gravelly Lake was later used for agricultural production.

1873 | Northern Pacific Railroad completes a line to Tacoma.

1908 | Emma Alexander purchases Lot 23 of Interlaaken Township and builds a small summer cabin on the five-acre property.

1914 | Streetcar lines are extended to Gravelly Lake, spurring the area's development as a retreat from the bustling city of Tacoma.

1918–1922 | Emma Alexander's son, H. F. Alexander, and his wife Ruth subsequently purchase an adjoining five-acre parcel and build a larger house, naming the ten-acre estate "Inglewood." The Brick Walk and Tea House are installed for the wedding of the Alexanders' daughter, Dorothy, to Joseph L. Carman Jr. in June of 1922.

1923 | Major Everett Griggs visits Tokyo after a catastrophic earthquake and returns with many statues, including Lakewold's stone lanterns and elephants, among others.

1925 | "Inglewood" is sold to Major Griggs and renamed "Lakewold," a Middle English word for a protected wooded glen.

1928 | First wisteria planted on what is now the Veranda at Lakewold.

1937 | Rena E. Wilbur breeds a fragrant, apricot-color climbing rose, naming it after Ruth Alexander; it is now growing on the kitchen wall.

1938–1940 | Lakewold is sold to Major Griggs's nephew, G. Corydon Wagner II and his wife Eulalie.

1949 | Dawn redwood planted, a tree considered extinct until its 1946 rediscovery in China.

1950s | Lion fountain, Sundial, and other statuary and pots acquired from the nearby Thornewood estate.

1958 | Thomas Church visits Lakewold as part of his first Pacific Northwest tour.

1958–1960s | William Platt and Thomas Church redesign the house and gardens.

1960s | Rose garden and Knot Garden planted.

1961 | Eighteenth-century hand-painted Chinese wallpaper acquired from Mallet, the London auction house, is installed in the entry of the house.

1962–1966 | Eulalie Wagner is a member of the Board of Directors for the Garden Club of America.

1970 | Parterre beds near sunroom installed.

1979 | Death of G. Corydon Wagner II (b. 1895).

1987 | Eulalie Wagner donates the estate to The Friends of Lakewold to steward the preservation of Lakewold Gardens.

1989 | Lakewold Gardens officially opens to the public on May 7.

1991 | Death of Eulalie Wagner (b. 1904).

1999 | Lakewold Gardens is officially declared a Historic Site by the Washington State Office of Archaeology and Historic Preservation.

2009 | Twentieth Anniversary of Lakewold Gardens. More than a quarter million visitors from around the world since 1989. Award-winning documentary, *Lakewold, Where the Blue Poppy Grows*, is digitally remastered and re-released on DVD.

2011 | Publication of *Lakewold: A Magnificent Northwest Garden.*

INTRODUCTION
Valerie Easton

I first visited Lakewold on a field trip with a group of cohorts from the University of Washington. I'd recently been hired as a horticultural librarian for the Elisabeth C. Miller Library, and I was anxious to come up to speed at my new job by learning the names of the many unusual plants at Lakewold. I've surely forgotten most of the botanical names I crammed into my head that day, but I'll never forget the sight of my first Ukon cherry tree (*Prunus serrulata* 'Ukon'). I hadn't a clue that yellow-blooming ornamental cherries even existed, and I was enthralled at the sight. The memory of that mature Ukon cherry, its soft yellow flowers set off by endless green lawns and the sparkling blue of Gravelly Lake, is as vivid as it was on that sunny April morning twenty-five years ago.

Such resounding yet intimate revelations of natural beauty are the wonders of Lakewold. I think just such experiences are what we long for most when we visit other people's gardens. Of course we lust after new and unusual plants, drink in the sense of place, glean design ideas. But the great lure and the joy of garden touring, the heart of the experience, is that moment when we breathe in something so new and fresh we go away dazzled. Such moments restore our sense of gardening as something more than tending our own little plot. For gardening is, and always has been, about reverence for the earth and celebrating nature's complexity and abundance. Spend even fifteen minutes at Lakewold and you know deep in your bones that the woman who created this masterpiece of a garden understood gardening in its most expansive sense.

Lakewold's pleasures are many, starting with its pronounced seasonality. Think of the unchanging evergreen nature of Japanese gardens, quietly beautiful in their way. Eulalie Wagner took quite a different tack in creating a garden that glorifies, even exaggerates, seasonal change.

TOP FROM LEFT: *Quercus garryana* (Oregon white oak, Garry oak) is native to the West Coast from Oregon to British Columbia. Shorter than its eastern cousins, its commercial value is secondary to the great aesthetic interest it provides in the garden, where its twisted growth pattern gives it an extraordinary winter silhouette.

In the Pacific Northwest, *R. augustinii* is a trouble free, moderately sized shrub. Its small, lavender blue flowers are the closest to a true blue that rhododendrons offer, making it an indispensable element in a sunny mixed border.

BOTTOM FROM LEFT: *Clerodendrum trichotomum* (Glory bower) is a fragrant, late-summer blooming small tree. Its white, jasmine-like flowers develop an even more striking display as the flowers fade and the electric blue seeds, accented by the fuschia pink calyxes, appear. Clerodendrum is also known as the Peanut butter bush, since its leaves, when crushed, have a similar fragrance.

This *Acer palmatum dissectum* 'Goshiki Shidare' (Japanese maple) was a gift to Mrs. Wagner from her sister, Virginia Bloedel, and was placed beneath the side of the wolf tree nearest the Wagner house. Mrs. Wagner chose to plant it there so that she could see it each morning from her bedroom window.

lakewold

Despite the looming green presence of shaggy native conifers, Lakewold in winter is all about the starkly sculptural quality of bare trees. When the leaves drop, the bones of the garden are revealed in bark, limb, and lichen. Witch hazels, snowdrops, and viburnum bloom through the coldest months, along with the early flowering pink *Rhododendron mucronulatum*. Toward winter's end, cyclamen, trillium, primulas, and dog's tooth violets (*Erythronium oregonum*) carpet the woodland.

Spring is Lakewold's quintessential season, for more than nine hundred big old rhododendrons burst into bedazzling bloom. The venerable copper beeches (predating the Wagners' time at Lakewold) leaf out, and the fresh foliage of Japanese maples lends a chartreuse, burgundy, and shrimp-toned haze to the garden.

Some of these trees are the biggest and oldest in Washington State, so you can imagine how the sheer plenitude of their unfurling leaves adds to the juiciness of springtime. Then there are the creamy Ukon cherries, the pink-blooming Mt. Fujis, the fragrant white and purple wisteria lacing the length of the terrace's pergola. Hedged parterres, filled with 'Angelique' tulips during Mrs. Wagner's time, now bloom with masses of crocus and narcissus.

The longer days of summer bring a lush, predominantly green palette to the lakeside estate. The traditional choice of annuals like zonal geraniums and begonias that at one time filled the parterres in summer has been replaced with a loose, colorful mix of cottage garden perennials. The knot garden is at its best in midsummer with its little herbal hedges, lavender, teucrium, and culinary herbs grouped around an old English stone wishing well.

Autumn brings a blaze of color from maples, oaks, beeches, birches, stewartia, and parrotia. Fruit not yet plundered by the birds hangs heavy on the *Cornus mas* and *Cornus kousa*. The Japanese maples in the woodland garden burn in sunset shades of gold and orange, and even we Northwesterners, so enamored of evergreens, can't help but be impressed by the splendor deciduous trees bring to the fall landscape.

By the 1950s, after developing the gardens for more than a decade, the Wagners longed to create more harmony between house and garden. It was Mrs. Wagner's idea to work from the inside out, hiring architects to redesign her manor house to suit the gardens instead of the other way around. The architects even replaced the home's exterior wood cladding with brick chosen to compliment the color of a favorite rhododendron, *R. williamsianum*. They also opened the austere and elegant old house up to the garden with a sunroom and a long, wisteria-drenched terrace. Despite the home's size, its roofline appears to hunker down peacefully into the landscape. The big

OPPOSITE: Earlier photographs of the parterres show that the plantings were never constant, but tulips were often used for a grand spring display. Yellow, white, and the double pink tulip 'Angelique' (above and left) were favorites. Over four thousand bulbs are needed to plant all the parterres. With its horizontal habit, the *Prunus serrulata* 'Shirotae' (Mt. Fuji cherry) is one of the most valuable architectural trees for a garden.

RIGHT: The glass is solid, of course, but its transparency provides a psychological sense that there is no barrier between interior and exterior space; the interior room adjoins the exterior room. Interior plants, such as the trailing hoya, complete the effect. From within the sunroom visitors can gain a strong sense of the complex elements of both the shade garden and the formal garden before experiencing them directly.

OPPOSITE, CLOCKWISE FROM LEFT: Thomas Church is noted for creating the concept of garden "rooms." In designing the circular driveway that lies just beyond the fringe of these trees and shrubs, he made the approach to the house subtle and seductive. He also created this spacious room for the west lawn, one that is in perfect harmony with the scale of the surrounding trees. At the right edge of this photograph is a *Paulownia tomentosa* (Empress tree, Foxglove tree, Princess tree), whose lilac flowers are shaped like the foxglove's. Standing in the north quadrant of the west lawn, it is a wonderful specimen tree.

The east terrace, terminated by the knot garden on the south end, runs the entire length of the Wagner house. Shown here without furniture, the terrace also serves as a transition between the house and its garden space. A glass roof above, along with regular pruning below, keeps the wisteria under control. See page 45 for a close-up of the wisteria.

Perhaps the most remarkable thing about this *Prunus serrulata* 'Ukon' (Ukon cherry) is the color of its blossoms. Borne in clusters of three to six double flowers, they are pale yellow on the outside with touches of pink on the petal edges.

old conifers, the house, and the Thomas Church–designed elements of the garden exist in a comfortable accord that adds to, rather than detracts, from the spirit and setting of the place.

Of all Lakewold's many takeaway lessons, the ultimate one must be its serenity. The formal gazebo, brick walkway, and quatrefoil pool somehow segue seamlessly to naturalistic woodland. Plantings strictly encircled by parterres transition smoothly to quieter scenes, like the ancient Shinto priest squatting in the shade garden beneath the wolf tree. Why does the eye wander so easily from Tommy Church formality to the modernity of native plants sweeping down to the shore of the lake? Tranquility may not have been the goal of a plant collector like Mrs. Wagner, yet her garden remains infused with a timeless quality. Perhaps it's because no matter how many plants she collected, from rhodies to alpines, she prized simplicity above all.

But we can't leave the subject of Lakewold's lessons without homing in on Church and Wagner's mastery of scale. The garden teaches us that the height and girth of our native trees—always a challenge in Northwest gardens both blessed and cursed with giant conifers—can be elegantly balanced with large enough expanses of lawn.

Lakewold's magnificent setting and the involvement of famous designers like Tommy Church, and perhaps the Olmsteds, have certainly shaped the garden's success. Is it the comfortable scale of Tommy Church's garden rooms, the harmony between informal and formal elements, the stunning size of the heritage trees, that make Lakewold so captivating? I think not, though all these contribute to its unique beauty. I believe that I, who stood rapt staring at that creamy cherry tree, shared a response felt by many visitors who respond viscerally to this garden: a sense of how deeply it has been shaped by Mrs. Wagner's devotion, skill, and hard work for more than thirty years. It remains one woman's personal garden, a living, growing record of her devotion to place and plants.

I can't help but think it would have brought great joy to Eulalie Wagner to know that so many visitors wander Lakewold enchanted by the ponds and waterfall, inhaling the lemony scent of magnolia blossoms, marveling over the tiny treasures in her scree garden. For a woman who examined her entire estate daily and knew all her plants by name, there can be no immortality more satisfying than having other gardeners following in her footsteps, and appreciating her flowers.

chapter one

LAKEWOLD: FROM THE BEGINNING
Ronald Fields

Gates play on two important elements for the imagination: invitation and exclusion. In this photograph from about 1915, Inglenook's handsome iron gate opens to reveal Mrs. Alexander, poised on a rustic settee. The gate is opened for the viewer to join her but the distance we feel, both psychological and physical, does not convey a sense of warm welcome. During the Griggs era, the gateposts were topped with light fixtures. Today they sport cast-stone eagles.

Northwest gardens are relatively young; our historically important examples are mere centenarians. Nevertheless, they do reflect the optimism and the expansive prosperity for which the Alaska-Yukon-Pacific Exposition of 1909, held in Seattle, stands witness. Washington had gained statehood in 1889. Sixteen years later Emma Alexander purchased the first parcel of what would become Lakewold Gardens; by 1914 she had expanded the property to its present ten acres and built a permanent home. She called the estate Inglewood.

The Alexander house was in the shingle style, reminiscent of the work of the American architect H. H. Richardson, which offered an elegant informality for country or resort living. And the Interlaken Township, as it was then known, was a resort area for those who could afford residences on its various lakes. In company with Inglewood were a half dozen other estate homes and gardens—the nationally known Thornewood was much larger, with vast terraced gardens designed by the Olmsted Brothers firm, and also the nearby forty-acre Madera estate—their plantings now vanished in the encroachment of residential development.

Local newspaper accounts gave great praise to the Alexander garden, reporting that "Nature-loving Tacomans make modern Arcady of Gravelly Lake's shores." [Among the plants of the Alexander garden are] . . . "tulip trees, mountain ash, silver poplars and flowering fruit trees and a rare collection of shrubbery. English laurel, rhododendrons, a hardy orange tree, palms and many choice shrubs of southern and imported varieties." – *Tacoma Daily Ledger*, November 30, 1913, p. 43.

"Surrounded in gorgeous gardens that during the spring and summer months are almost tropical in their luxuriance and bloom, 'Inglewood,' the rustic and cozy country home of the Alexanders, is one of the beauty spots on the Gravelly Lake shore." – *Tacoma Daily Ledger*, July 23, 1916, p. 26.

"Nature-loving Tacomans make modern Arcady of Gravelly Lake's shores."
— *Tacoma Daily Ledger,* 1913

LEFT: Emma Alexander and her daughter-in-law, Ruth, ca. 1920.

RIGHT: Emma Alexander on the brick walkway. Note the enormous English-style borders on each side of the walkway that run its entire length. Mrs. Wagner and Mr. Church later chose to replace these high-maintenance beds with parterres.

Major Everett Griggs purchased the Alexander property in 1925, at which time it acquired its name, Lakewold, and, a dozen years later, sold it to his nephew Mr. Corydon Wagner. It was under the guidance of Mrs. Corydon Wagner that the gardens came to be among the more celebrated on the Pacific coast.

Eulalie Merrill Wagner did not turn her complete attention to gardening until faced with a ten-acre canvas that held only a few established, but nevertheless important, features. In 1919, the Olmsted firm had provided a garden plan for the Alexanders that included the gazebo, a 235-foot brick walkway from the house to the gazebo, and the stone fence bordering the western side of the garden.[1] The brick walkway has served as a fundamental axis for the garden and has dominated every subsequent development in that area. The elaborate iron gate, acquired by the Alexanders, also dates from this period.

Along each side of the walkway at the gazebo entrance were large flower beds for roses and perennials. Attempting to maintain these against wind and rain proved to be futile. "I spent my youth," Mrs. Wagner said, "tying up phlox and delphinium."[2]

However inexperienced she may have been, she was not without exposure to wider possibilities. Her parents' garden was an outstanding one, professionally designed and including important antique Italian sculpture and fountains. And she was well traveled: Europe for months at a time, Japan and India. She had a keen eye for design, scale, and form, and she had the tenacity

"The immense variety of flora in her garden demanding diverse cultural conditions and their artful placement within were, for me, advanced lessons in design as well as horticulture."

— Alison Andrews, a Seattle friend of Mrs. Wagner

LEFT: Arching over the stone fence, the white *Viburnum plicatum f. tomentosum* (Doublefile viburnum) was a significant identifying feature of the property for decades, until an overzealous gardener removed it. The garden has suffered other casualties, too, as when the swimming pool was once filled with stones, and when rare camellias near the knot garden were taken out in following a staff member's short-sighted plans. Fortunately, the strength of the garden design and its core fabric of plants protect it from being irreparably harmed by such events.

"Regarding things she really wanted, protocol did not stand in her way. Once we found in our modest garden a very rare and expensive plant that replaced one she had removed the night before. She just wanted our plant, though less expensive, to enhance some plantings of hers." — Corydon Wagner III

to seriously study horticulture, a preoccupation that stayed with her for the rest of her life. She must have known she needed to be rescued from the endless summer hours those large beds of perennials demanded.

Thomas Church began his work with Mrs. Wagner in 1958. On his initial visit, he gave advice on what was to become a surprisingly odd yet fundamental feature of the gardens: a shade garden beneath a misshapen Douglas fir called a wolf tree. After having thinned it so light could reach the floor, and creating pebble paths around the trunk, she placed a very old statue of a Shinto priest beside a small reflecting pool at one entrance and a *yukimi* style snow lantern at the other (both had been acquired in Japan by Major Griggs), and planted a variety of early blooming, low-growing plants. "On drizzly spring mornings," she writes, "the first rhododendron blossoms could be admired from the inside, in my glass-enclosed garden room. No one needs to wander far from the house to view cyclamen, cypripedium (lady slipper orchids), bloodroot . . . hellebores."[3] It became one of her favorite sections of the garden.

Lakewold was still heavily wooded. To create the signature garden rooms for which he was noted, Church had numerous two-hundred-year old fir trees removed. The original driveway, running rather straight from the street to the porte cochere at the front door, was redirected into a sweeping arc that gives glimpses of one's destination through a variety of trees and rhododendrons, ending in a low-walled motor court for as many as twenty cars—a room in itself, edged in statuary and urns, and flanked by styrax, dogwood, camellias, and flowering cherries.

succeeded in establishing the fern *Polypodium scouleri* (Leathery polypody) in the branches of the wolf tree, so that it would appear as it naturally does on trees in the Olympic Mountains.

Seriously damaged in the 1991 ice storm, this flowering cherry, *Prunus serrulata whitcombii*, was removed. In its place now stands a Korean dogwood, *Cornus kousa* 'Satomi'.

The shade garden beneath the wolf tree contains a wide variety of early heralds of spring—hellebores, bloodroot, trillium, and cyclamen. In summer, the interest shifts to enjoyment of the differing textures and patterns of foliage.

OPPOSITE: The water garden lies east of the wolf tree and stretches the entire length of the slope to the lake shore. It was designed by Mr. John Fischer and executed by Mr. Steve Balint in 1966. The huge stones came from the Cascade Mountains. The water, pumped up from Gravely Lake, returns to it through a series of small pools and falls. Because this garden is never in full sun, native maidenhair ferns, leather ferns, and other shade-loving plants abound here.

With Mr. Church's help, the labor-intensive perennial beds at the gazebo gave way to parterres. The swimming pool, with its flanking, low brick wall, became another room, forming a cross axis to the brick walkway terminated by a lion fountain and a sundial. Mr. Church made yearly visits to the garden, creating formal additions, and always engaged in discussions about other garden projects that were never formally drafted. For example, the removal of trees on the east lawn to create a rockery was the result of a Friday discussion; the chain saws arrived the next day to execute the plan.[4]

He and Mrs. Wagner did not always see eye to eye. She wanted a water element; he opposed it. With the help of Mr. John Fischer and Steve Balint, she got her water garden: a series of pools and falls tucked away in a sloping wooded area now immersed in rare maples, native plants, and rhododendrons. The massive stones were brought from the Cascade Mountains, and she supervised their placement. Inspired by a grotto in Lisbon, she created a misted fern marsh at the head of her water garden, and near its base, at a viewpoint to the lake, she created three small, dry scree gardens.

The defining plant feature of her garden is the rhododendron collection. Beginning with hybrids, she quickly became enamored of the much rarer and more difficult-to-maintain species. The Rhododendron Species Foundation (with the assistance of Mr. Wagner) was moved from its Oregon location to just a few miles north of the Lakewold gardens. She worked with the foundation and became acquainted with local growers and breeders, but she also traveled to England many times to select specimens both for the foundation and for her own garden. Yet the rarity of a plant was not the defining reason for its presence in her garden. Her garden was a living palette of color, texture, and scale. She didn't hesitate to relocate sizeable plants from place to place to satisfy her sense of design.

Under her care, Lakewold became several gardens—formal, rock, scree, shade, water, woodland, cutting, and herb. It has classical as well as modern elements. Even as its bones became

firmly established, her vision for it continued to evolve as new genera were
introduced and subtle exchanges evolved in annual and perennial bedding areas.
Mrs. Wagner came to enjoy the challenge of "That plant will not flourish here"
and prove that it could. She could (and did) tinker with Mother Nature by
creating microenvironments or, on occasion, postponing the maturation of a tulip
bed by icing it down. She knew all her plants by name, and daily examined the
entire estate.

She wrote:

*Mr. Church's annual visits, along with his books, were a continuous
education for me. His requisites for a garden may be iterated in four:
function, continuity, simplicity and scale. First and foremost, my garden
must be functional. My driveway and parking area must be adequate for all
occasions. There must be continuity, with one section flowing into another,
and a visual transition beyond. Above all, I learned about simplicity. This,
I feel, has been achieved, as the garden has acquired an aura of tranquility
which I hope is shared by all. Last but not least, the scale of the garden
must conform to our gigantic, indigenous trees, thus the large expanses of
lawn are most appropriate.*

*I realize some people are uncontrollable collectors, for I am one of them.
During the past forty years, I have moved through phases, my first being
rhododendrons, which I've never really given up. . . . Next came my
penchant for roses, then an Elizabethan knot garden of culinary herbs,
patterned geometrically around an antique wellhead from England that I
purchased at auction; then maple trees, cherries, and on and onward until
finally my last and most absorbing hobby is the alpine plants in my rockery,
to which there is no end.*[5]

In 1998, this "aura of tranquility" was made historical fact by the selection
of Lakewold Gardens to the prestigious international roster of Gardens for Peace;
Lakewold was the fifth to be selected; only sixteen have so far been named.

RIGHT: Thomas Church in the Wagner sunroom, 1974.

OPPOSITE TOP: There are many varieties of *R. williamsianum.* All are characterized by rounded leaves and trusses of loose, pendulous blossoms. 'Bow Bells' was a particular favorite of Mrs. Wagner, and this plant received its place of honor in a cartouche above the front door of the Wagner house. As one stands in the front court, one sees the soft pink brick of the house, and pink abounds in the surrounding dogwoods, camellias, and rhododendrons.

OPPOSITE BOTTOM: *Trillium sessile* (sometimes called Toadshade or Wake robin) is valued more for its foliage than for its flower. A native of the eastern United States, its deep red blossoms have no stem and emerge directly from the leaf. The native western trillium has its own stem, which gives it a more nodding effect.

LEFT: Thomas Church began his work at Lakewold in 1958. His advice was not limited to the designs that came from his drafting table, and until Mr. Wagner's death in 1978 he visited the Wagner family every year. He would arrive on a Friday, he and Mr. and Mrs. Wagner would formulate ideas for additional treatments, and on Saturday crews would promptly arrive to execute them. This overlook was one of their ideas, and permits reluctant guests seated here to view the water features without walking down the embankment.

In 1998, this element of Lakewold was placed on the list of Gardens for Peace, an International Network of Gardens to Promote Peace.

RIGHT: This figure, the Gatherer, along with her partner the Hunter (see page 61), stands on the wall of the automobile court; together they are nearly life-size, and bracket the opening to the west lawn.

NOTES

1 *Eulalie*, VHS 712.6, Seattle Public Library, John Robinson (interviewer)and Donald Schmechel, 1986. In an oral history project sponsored by the Seattle Public Library, Mrs. Wagner tells John Robinson that the Olmsted plans for the garden had been found, and that they included the stone fence and the *Viburnum tomentosum* that flanked it. Mrs. Alexander's granddaughter-in-law, Mrs. Joseph L. Carman III, reported that it had always been a family assumption that the Olmsted firm had contributed to the garden design, and that the brick walk had been copied from an Olmsted walkway at nearby Thornewood; Interview 2-12-2010.

Major Griggs, too, had business with the Olmsted firm. From 1909 to 1923 he corresponded with the company involving surveys and plans for property he owned on nearby American Lake. Photocopies of the Library of Congress original letters are in the Carman family papers and the Wagner family papers.

2 Ibid.

3 Manuscript in the Wagner Home papers, p. 4. This speech was probably written for a presentation to the Garden Club of America, 1977, when the club was visiting Lakewold.

4 Interview with Steve Balint, former gardener for the Lakewold Estate, 2-16-2010.

5 Wagner Home papers, p. 8.

Lakewold Gardens Photographic Tour

Promptly at ten each morning Mrs. Wagner would meet with her gardeners and walk through the gardens with them, pointing out the tasks she wished to see accomplished for the day. We may be charmed by the scatter of magnolia blossoms, but clearing them away was likely one of the tasks of the garden crew.

RIGHT: Garden sculptures often recognize that gardening is ruled by the passing seasons. This figure, with her basket of blossoms, exemplifies the goddess Flora, goddess of flowers and spring, as well as thoughts that turn toward love in that season.

PREVIOUS PAGE: Geographically, Lakewold's location is described as a prairie, an environment in which large stones are not found. These stones for the water garden were brought down from the nearby Cascade Mountains and are so harmoniously incorporated with native and imported vegetation as to appear perfectly natural.

Mrs. Griggs planted the first wisteria at Lakewold. The present plants (the specific cultivar is unknown) were put in place when the terrace was constructed. A glass roof, held up by iron supports, helps control the plants' tendril growth; it also protects the terrace furniture and Mrs. Wagner's collection of lewisias from heavy rain.

Crocus provided the earliest color to appear in the parterres at the south end of the brick walk, often in blue to suggest a pond for the water birds. This is an early image of the parterres, showing the intricacy of their detail; in later years the pattern was simplified, allowing for less intensive trimming of the boxwood.

PREVIOUS PAGES: Thomas Church discouraged the development of the water garden, feeling that it would present the problem of too intensive maintenance. He warned Mrs. Wagner that she would inevitably spend all her time in the rockery while his "beautiful, formal garden turned into a shambles."

Most of the garden paths converge on picnic point, but each is surrounded by a garden of its own. Plantings found at the edge of the path may vary from small alpines and ground covers in open areas, to spring bulbs and ferns in more shaded spaces. These smaller elements are backed by azaleas, rhododendrons, and native plants.

Specimen trees include the *Embothrium coccineum* (Chilean flame tree), *Davidia involucrata* (Dove tree), *Fagus sylvatica* 'Purpurea tricolor' (Tricolor beech), *Parrotia persica* (Persian ironwood), and numerous Japanese maples.

For twenty years, this large scree, located near the lakeside edge of the east lawn, was a labor of love for Mrs. Wagner. Perhaps because they are a challenge to grow in the Northwest climate, collecting alpine plants became one of her passions.

The scree garden is intended to emulate an alpine or mountain moraine where erosion and weather have broken down rock ridges into small, pea-sized gravel mixed with limited organic matter. A scree must have quick drainage as the small plants native to high altitudes will not tolerate "wet feet."

"The immense variety of flora in her garden demanding diverse cultural conditions and their artful placement within were, for me, advanced lessons in design as well as horticulture. The many vistas throughout the garden encouraged, even demanded, a closer look, and the paths to the lake were a wondrous journey rather than just a means to an end." – Alison Andrews, a Seattle friend of Mrs. Wagner and an accomplished gardener

Many of the plants in this knot garden are Mediterranean in origin, requiring hot and rather dry conditions for good health. By contrast, the Northwest climate is cool and damp, conditions that only an expert gardener can overcome.

In his teens, Mrs. Wagner's grandson Cordy Ryman enjoyed working in the garden and pleased her enormously by trimming the boxwood with his thumbnail and forefinger, eliminating the brown edges and sharp lines produced by shears.

Bacchus, the god of wine, is also associated with autumn, the season of harvest. The presence of personifications of the seasons has a long tradition in gardens, reminding us that all garden activities are ruled by the four seasons.

The Hunter stands at the opening between the automobile court and the west lawn. He and his female partner, the Gatherer, are each sheltered by a white-flowering *Styrax japonicus* (Japanese snowbell), which bears tiny, bell-shaped white flowers in late spring.

"Divers must be satisfied with jumping off the raised flower boxes, for a board and a ladder would have been foreign to this scene."

— Thomas Church

The swimming pool presents an optical illusion. It is forty feet wide, yet the inset points with their containers of plants visually reduce its scale, making it appear smaller. The pool was one of Mr. Church's favorite achievements, and he used an image of it on the cover of his book, *Gardens Are for People*. He also incorporated a variation of this same floral or quatrefoil pattern in the design for the floor of the gazebo.

The Wagner house reveals two quite
different personalities. The west facade,
designed by William Platt, is a geometric
cube, reminiscent of the central block
found in Georgian architecture. Its rigid
authority stands in direct contrast to the
lush vegetation on each side. In fact, the
flanking shrubs and trees disguise the
fact that the house extends both to the
left and right of the central block. From
the outside edges, shrubs taper down to
give emphasis to the entrance, and the
visual interest created by the windows
and shutters at the eave softens the
unexpected absence of windows at the
first story level.

The east side of the house is much more integrated with the garden. From the garage wall at the south end, laced with a kiwi (*Actinidia kolomikta* 'Arctic Beauty') and rose vines, through the terraced central section covered with wisteria, to the north sunroom there is no sharp distinction between house and garden. The expanse of large windows reinforces the harmonious relationship of house to garden.

When this Douglas fir was about five feet tall, its apical or terminal bud was somehow broken. Lateral buds shot out from the main stem, creating a sprawling habit. In the wild it would be virtually useless for lumber and dangerous for the lumberjack, and for that reason it is sometimes called a "widow maker" as well as a "wolf tree."

Typically a wolf tree inhibits the growth of smaller trees around it. Lakewold's wolf tree is a testament to this statement. Fortunately many smaller plants can thrive in this somewhat inhospitable ecological zone. Ephemerals, plants that emerge very quickly in late winter or early spring, flower, go to seed, and disappear for the remainder of the year, find a very pleasant home under the wolf tree. To venture into the garden at this time of year is to discover spring ephemerals like *Trillium sessile* and *T. ovatum*, erythronium, sanguinaria, and hepatica, plants that are warmly awaited as harbingers of spring. The wonderful canopy of the wolf tree provides the visitor and these delightful charmers a protected place to enjoy the most modest season at Lakewold.

chapter TWO

THE MUSIC OF A GRAND GARDEN
Steve Lorton

A garden is a performing art. Like a symphony, it is the product of its composer, who often conducts the early performances. Such was the case with Lakewold. Eulalie Merrill Wagner was both composer and conductor from 1938 until her death in 1991.

Works of art are best understood if something is known about their creators. Born in the early twentieth century (1904), Mrs. Wagner entered a world of wealth unimaginable to most of us. And while the term "aristocrat" is inapplicable to Americans, she was brought up in much the same way as a titled European. She was schooled in fine art and architecture, the domestic and decorative arts, history and the classics. Her family traveled regularly to the cultural pockets of the American East Coast and to Europe. They lived in Paris while Eulalie's childhood home, Merrill House on Seattle's Capitol Hill, was being built. In retrospect she would see herself as both a product of Europe's Belle Epoch and the American Gilded Age.

Eulalie Wagner had a keen sense of the difference between fashion and style and was a master of both. She cultivated artists and designers, admiring them, surrounding herself with

Mrs. Wagner took care to have her gardens in pristine condition for her parties. Dale Bobb, who was a temporary summer garden helper while attending high school, reports that one of his duties was to take freshly cut grass and sprinkle it on any scalped spots left by the lawn mowers. For the duration of the party, the lawn would appear immaculate. — Dale Bobb, DDS, Tacoma

In this east view across the swimming pool, a small Queen Anne sundial lies in a direct axis line with the pool. Beyond it, Mount Rainier can be seen through an opening in the wooded area beyond.

Eulalie Wagner arrived at Lakewold in 1938, taking over what was merely a sketch of a score for her symphonic garden. The long brick walk leading to the rose-covered gazebo was in place. The grand stone and wood fence that flanks the roadside edge of the property was there, and thankfully a stand of virgin Douglas fir had been left along with the signature Garry oaks of the Tacoma area. She went to work.

Mrs. Wagner learned by trial and error. Inside the boxwood parterres she planted a spectacular display of spring bulbs. As they faded, a kaleidoscope of perennials popped up for summer bloom. But June rains made them flop to the ground. Quick to learn and respond, Mrs. Wagner replaced the perennials with sturdy, floriferous, long-blooming, and low-to-the-ground displays of annuals in gorgeous color combinations. Impatiens was a favorite. She changed the show annually.

She also understood the value of getting good advice. In the 1950s, renowned landscape architect Thomas Church entered the picture (you can read about him in the next chapter). His commission, and the friendship that ensued between the Wagners and the Churches, lasted a lifetime. His impact on the garden was enormous. As a cutting-edge designer who loved the easygoing simplicity of western life, Church also knew his client and conjured his horticultural sorcery in exploiting both the classical grandeur of the garden (and its creator) and the obstreperous nature of the Northwest wilderness. When Mr. Wagner needed a lap pool for exercise, Church designed the symmetrical, four-lobed pool with its low, planted pillars that serves as a focal point today. It is both beautiful and functional.

Close to the middle of the garden stands a multi-trunked Douglas fir. Useless for lumber, it is what loggers call a "wolf tree." Mrs. Wagner pondered what to do about it. Cut it down? Limb it up? Church looked at it and said, "Feature it!"

Today that venerable tree stands proud in the garden, encircled by a walk-through shade garden. For many years a mother mallard made her way, about five and half feet up to the first outcropping of its trunks, to build her nest and raise her young. To Mrs. Wagner's delight the mother duck squawked with authority when any visitor, herself included, strolled past the nest as they studied the shade garden.

As revered as Church was, however, his counsel was only that . . . an opinion offered. When he nixed the idea of the rockery, Mrs. Wagner forged ahead nonetheless. And isn't any visitor today happy she did?

ABOVE, LEFT TO RIGHT: One of three stone containers from China acquired by Major Griggs

Dr. Luke Li, of Beijing University, writes: "The patterns of the middle section show the stylistic features from the West Region in China (symmetrical acanthus design, wavy line, posy pattern, and paired animal). Its composition is dynamic. The image of the lion indicates that it comes from the post-Yuan period (after 1368 AD). The upper, middle, and lower parts of it have several styles of floral patterns, with a different degree of fineness. It is difficult to tell when and where it was made, in [the] Fujian and Guangzhou region (Southeast China), or possibly in another part of Asia." – translation by Zaixin Hong, PhD, University of Puget Sound

This is one of a pair of musical satyrs now in the pool area; both are about four feet high. They were brought to the garden by Major Griggs and were originally placed in the gazebo.

This elephant, with succulents, is also one of a pair. These little planters, just twenty-one inches high, reside in the library court.

When the Tacoma Garden Club began studying scree, it resulted in the Gray Scree at Lakewold as well as the scree at the Tacoma Garden Club Northwest Native Plant Garden in Point Defiance Park. The Wagner Family provided the funds for a handsome gazebo at the foot of the scree so that visitors could sit there and contemplate both its simplicity and its intricacy. A contradiction of terms? No. Go see the scree.

And when you go, witness yet another manifestation of Eulalie Wagner's generosity and spirit of public service.

Once I visited the garden with the renowned British garden designer and author, Rosemary Verey. Rosemary eyeballed the statue of Bacchus standing under the lattice dome of the Tea House. "Isn't he beautiful!" Rosemary commented, hoping for a history and a possible price tag.

Mrs. Wagner nodded, "Beautiful. Yes, I think so." Then Rosemary's eye went to a trio of stone fish resting at the bottom of a stone vessel filled with water. "Oh! How beautiful! May I pick one up?" Her British accent was shrill and punctuated.

"Of course," Mrs. Wagner responded.

"Just what is the stone?" Rosemary asked.

"Jade," Mrs. Wagner answered dryly.

And so it went. As we drove back to Seattle, Rosemary carried on about how lovely the garden was and how much she enjoyed the visit and how she found Eulalie "captivating," later comparing her to an English Country Lady. High marks, one would suppose, from the maven of British gardening who helped Prince Charles design Highgrove. I doubt that Mrs. Wagner thought about the visit again.

My hunch is that the great Rosemary Verey was so impressed with that very fine garden, so surprisingly paired with the woman who stood behind it in an unassuming American way, that it rattled her British sensibilities. The garden seems to encompass a multitude of styles and periods, with room to spare, a manifestation of the enormity and the eclecticism of our country. Something, I suspect, the British envy deeply and regret losing.

Like the scree, the Mount Fuji Cherry trees, the Fern Garden, the Waterfall (so real you can't believe a pump is behind it), the Herb Garden with its English well, which I say (and remember hearing) is Spanish . . . all of these are inimitable movements in the symphony that this composer produced and, for so long, conducted. In flower, leaf, color, and form she produced allegros and andantes, crescendos and arpeggios, surrounded by ancient Northwest conifers that could rumble like timpani in a gust of wind.

The Wagner grandchildren often scrambled into the lower branches of the wolf tree for summer adventure. The Wagners' youngest daughter, Merrill, also enjoyed the wolf tree as one of her favorite summer reading spots.

chapter three

CHURCH IN THE WOODS
Marc Treib

I n 1958, when "Tommie" Church began to consult on the landscape design of Lakewold, he already reigned as America's premier landscape architect. For over twenty years his work had enjoyed extensive publication in professional and popular journals such as *House Beautiful*. His first book, *Gardens Are for People* (1955), assembled a compendium of his realized projects and further disseminated his ideas on contemporary garden design to a national and even international audience.[1]

Thomas Dolliver Church (1902–1978) graduated from the University of California, Berkeley, in 1922, and, after a year of study in Europe supported by a traveling scholarship, completed a master's degree at Harvard University in 1927. The primary subjects of his study were the landscapes of the Mediterranean and their possible application to new landscapes in California. Given their analogous climate—and what he perceived to be similar topography and vegetation—Italy, France, and Spain provided a viable model.[2] As it happens, few of Church's landscapes employed the grand Mediterranean manner of old, but many drew upon classical forms, especially in his early and later years. Between them lay a series of landmark works that danced with modernist imagery. Church was hardly dogmatic about style, however, and after working at both stylistic extremes he eventually accepted an eclectic practice that incorporated both.

Thomas Church, 1975

A view of the knot garden, showing the steps at the south end of the terrace.

Parterres are first an overall geometric design, resting calmly in a designated space. Close observation reveals a rhythmic play of squares and circles, cubes, spheres, and spirals, combining into intricate patterns.

— Thomas Church

the house itself, as do the details Church used in the walls and paving designs. The elevation of the terrace also enhances the views of the lake although they are lateral rather than axial and partially obscured by the trunks of the trees.

Set within the terrace, the knot garden adds a bit of the whimsy characteristic of many Church gardens, in this case with sources tracing to Renaissance England. Here clipped forms intertwine in a symmetrical emblem. "Parterres," claimed Church in his second book, *Your Private World* of 1969, "are first an overall geometric design, resting calmly in a designated space. Close observation reveals a rhythmic play of squares and circles, cubes, spheres, and spirals, combining into intricate patterns."[9]

The intricacy of the knot garden resonates in the flower beds edged by evergreen boxwood. Sets of flower beds flank the central walkway running parallel to the main axis of the house, connecting the terrace with the pool and gazebo at its terminus. Bird forms executed in topiary grace the composition with a touch of humor—or some hint of wildlife, perhaps, when the birds themselves have flown. It is this area that most closely matches our traditional image of a garden: here are the beds and the flowers and the hedges, here are the colors and the fragrances and the textures changing more noticeably with the seasons.

The latticed gazebo at the end of the walk marks the limit of the garden, reinforced by masses of rhododendrons behind it. It is a later design, added in 1971. To one side of the path is the swimming pool, perhaps the most curious—and even contentious—element of the Lakewold garden landscape. As Church explained it, "[T]he wife wanted a pool in keeping with the simplicity and elegance of her traditional garden. So did her husband, but he is also a vigorous swimmer and did not wish to settle for a pool that would curb his enjoyment of the sport."[10] Church's solution

RIGHT: Knot Garden plans A and B.

OPPOSITE: The exterior square with its concave corners is bounded by dwarf boxwood. In the photo, the boxwood has not yet formed a continuous wall. The inner square is probably germander (Mr. Church suggested green santolina, then lined it through); the pale green arcs are gray santolina. Other plant suggestions included dwarf polyanthus roses (red 'Happy', pink 'Fairy', white 'Charlie McCarthy', or a mixed group), as well as boxwood globes and boxwood pyramids and azaleas on standards. Ground-cover suggestions were primroses, violas, and dwarf campanula.

All available photographs indicate that Mrs. Wagner took his recommendations for the framework but ignored his suggestions for filler plants. Her preference was for herbs: varieties of oregano, lavender, lemon balm, and mint (planted in their plastic containers so as not to spread), all selected for both color and texture. The knot garden appears somewhat smaller than its actual dimensions of twenty by twenty feet.

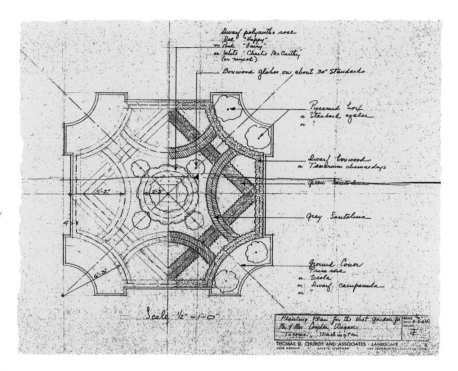

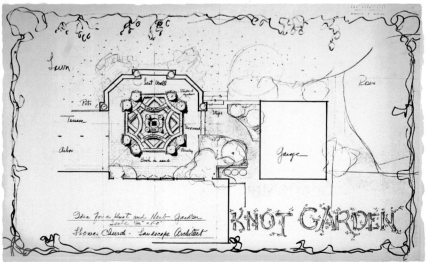

ABOVE: Attached to the left side of the gazebo, and partially below ground level, the dressing room for swimmers is inconspicuous. Equally unnoticeable is the small kitchenette (right) hidden by vegetation. The Wagner family often had lunch in the gazebo during warm weather. The kitchenette also provided space for caterers and bartenders serving the frequent large parties the Wagner's hosted.

LEFT: The floor within the gazebo shows a variation of the quatrefoil pattern of the swimming pool. The latticework on the right side hides a sliding door to the kitchenette; today the area has been converted for wheelchair-accessible facilities.

Church blended the existing mixed vegetation with magnolias and dogwoods, interweaving and articulating the old with new plantings that in some ways set off the older vegetation and in other ways complemented it.

was a quatrefoil shape that from most points in the garden appeared as a decorative basin but was actually large enough to permit swimming: "Its derivation from early classic forms fits into the existing scene, and 40 feet of length in two directions keeps the swimmers happy." Vegetation planted at each intersection of the four cusps was allowed to overflow, softening the geometric lines of the pool. There was no diving board: "Divers must be satisfied with jumping off the raised flower boxes, for a board and a ladder would have been foreign to this scene," stated Church.[11] Yet unlike his pool designs in later gardens, here Church left the lining of the pool white, producing a brilliant aqua color, which, before it was changed, troubled the harmony of the landscape as a whole.

While we can talk of these elements individually, it is their coherence as a thoroughly integrated work that transcends their independent identities. Lakewold's success lies in its reading as a whole, as an integrated landscape that shows few signs of its having benefited from the landscape architect's designs and advice over a period of some twenty years, and developed for forty more years thereafter. Today, those plantings suggested by Church have matured and blended with the vegetation that had predated the designer's intervention, to the point where we no long distinguish, or even care to distinguish, what is the work of nature and what is the work of the landscape architect, the clients, and the gardeners. Lakewold is far from being Thomas Church's most stridently modern or innovative landscape design, but it certainly ranks high among his most elegant and harmonious gardens.

Mr. Church once remarked that every garden needs a surprise element. This three-foot-high stump with its carving of three owls—so hidden in the wooded area that one can easily overlook it—was, for him, that "Ah ha!" discovery, and he referred to this little spot as the Surprise Garden.

When they first came to Lakewold both Mr. and Mrs. Wagner were avid competitive golfers. They practiced their shots in the area where the sundial now sits. Mr. Wagner had a small shed nestled into the shrubbery to house their clubs. She had more trophies than he, having won the Tacoma Country and Golf Club's Ladies' title four times. Then, in the mid-1950s, Mrs. Wagner shifted her attention from golf to her garden, winning honors there too. The Garden Club of America awarded her the Medal of Merit in 1968, the Montague Award in 1978, and, in 1984, the Creative Leadership Award and the Zone Horticultural Achievement Award.

NOTES

1   Thomas Church, *Gardens Are for People* (New York: Reinhold, 1955). A paperback third edition of 1995 was published by the University of California Press and remains in print.

2   Church's master's thesis was titled "A Study of Mediterranean Gardens and Their Adaptability to California Conditions" (master's thesis, Harvard University, 1927).

3   *Contemporary Landscape Architecture and Its Sources* (San Francisco: San Francisco Museum of Art, 1937); and the cover of *Sunset*, February 1937.

4   For a more detailed study of the landscape architect's life and work see Marc Treib, ed., *Thomas Church, Landscape Architect: Designing a Modern Californian Landscape* (San Francisco: William Stout Publishers, 2003).

5   A comprehensive study of this garden appears in Marc Treib, *The Donnell and Eckbo Gardens: Modern Californian Masterworks* (San Francisco: William Stout Publishers, 2005).

6   Church, *Gardens Are for People*, 216–18.

7   For an overview of the Bloedel Reserve, see Lawrence Kreisman, *The Bloedel Reserve: Gardens in the Forest* (Bainbridge Island, WA: The Arbor Fund, 1988); materials on Church's contribution are held in the Environmental Design Archives, University of California, Berkeley.

8   This historical background comes from Rita Happy, *Lakewold Gardens: Where the Blue Poppies Grow* (Tacoma, WA: Friends of Lakewold, n.d.).

9   Thomas Church, *Your Private World: A Study of Intimate Gardens* (San Francisco: Chronicle Books, 1969), 22.

10   Ibid., 140.

11   Ibid.

chapter four

RARE PLANTS
Katie Burki

Rare plants are those that are difficult to find because they are not in production, are seldom cultivated, or are scarce in the wild. Thus they are sought after not only for their rarity, but also for their horticultural value in species conservation and preservation. Rare plants also include varieties that are successfully cultivated in environments alien to their natural habitat. Avid gardeners and horticulturists have for centuries been in competition with their kin to obtain rare plants and thereby set themselves and their gardens apart from the less-successful collector or the prosaic garden. Fortunately it is a happy rivalry that has benefited all garden enthusiasts.

Mrs. Wagner had connections with nurseries and plantsmen throughout Washington, Oregon, and British Columbia. Through networking, Mrs. Wagner acquired rare plants that had never been released to the general trade (some Rhododendron breeders even named varieties for Wagner family members), and she obtained plants traded only among a few collectors in the Northwest. She

Discovered in 1945, the double flowered *Trillium ovatum* was propagated at the Bloedel Reserve, the home of Mrs. Wagner's sister on Bainbridge Island, Washington. Lakewold was one of the first gardens to receive a specimen and it has been in the wolf tree shade garden since 1950. Now available through specialty nurseries, it has been in the trade for several decades.

LEFT TOP: Like the linearifolias, rhododendrons are plants whose interest for much of the year is chiefly their foliage rather than their flower. The long, thin, dark green leaves of this *R. roxianum* var. 'Oreonastes' are its best feature. The flower clusters are relatively small.

LEFT: The rare *R. quinquefolium* is a little-known and underappreciated native of Japan. The pendulous, white, bell-like flowers are loosely sprinkled about the plant, unlike the customary tight trusses of the rhododendron. Lakewold's specimen is almost ten feet tall.

belonged to a number of rare plant societies, and she traveled widely. Mr. Wagner, a lumberman, also shared her interests in rare plants, but his focus was more closely directed toward trees.

> For those interested in Forestry, there is a collection of exotic species. My husband and I traveled around the world in 1953, and, in many places, visited arboretums and private forests where my husband obtained seeds and, in some cases, small trees. Upon our return, a conifer garden was started on the Northern slope. . . . A few examples are: *Abies pinsapo* (Spanish fir), *Pinus montana* (mugho), *Cunninghamia lanceolata* (China fir), *Pinus griffithii*, *Cedrus atlantica* 'Argentea' (Atlas cedar), *Taxodium distichum* (Bald cypress), and *Cupressus lusitanica* (Mexican cypress).[1]

In 1974, Lakeview Gardens, in Victoria, BC, then owned by the Lohbrunners, was preparing to close shop. The collection of alpine plants they had amassed in nearly half a century was internationally known, and was considered one of the best on this continent. The Lohbrunners, however, did not wish the collection to be divided and dispersed, so they were prepared to give the collection in its entirety to Lakewold. Mrs. Wagner did acquire ninety percent of the collection, and many of these plants still thrive in the garden today, most notably the native, though rarely cultivated *Vancouveria parviflora*.

Some rare plants were only disseminated to institutions like Lakewold, to insure their survival. For example, a rare, unnamed, double-flowered *Trillium ovatum* was discovered by Mrs. E. E. Weisenfluh on her Oregon property in 1945. The plant was obtained and cultivated by the Bloedel Reserve until enough clones could be created for wider distribution. Lakewold was one of five other Northwest institutions to acquire a specimen. While it has since been introduced into commercial production, the original specimen still grows at Lakewold.

Mrs. Wagner was also an avid collector of all Ericaceous plants, especially the rhododendron, as well as ferns and spring ephemerals. Although both the genera and species of these plants are much more readily available now, most of them were quite rare during her years at Lakewold. She was also a founding member of two local organizations, the Rhododendron Species Foundation and the Fern Foundation, whose formation and interest brought wider recognition to these plants; they also sought to bring more unusual plants into the trade. These foundations continue to thrive today, helping to introduce beautiful and unusual plants to both public and collectors' gardens throughout the world.

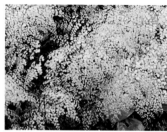

TOP: Growing in the large scree, this unknown species of the blue gentian was a favorite of Mrs. Wagner's. The texture of the petals is velvety, and their color is iridescent. Because it blooms in February, few visitors get to experience this lovely Alpine native.

ABOVE: Lakewold's fern garden is also a display garden for the Fern Foundation. Some seventy varieties of fern are found throughout the gardens, but the greatest concentration of them appears in this small, shaded space west of the sunroom. This evergreen Himalayan maidenhair fern, *Adiantum venustum*, is rare because it cannot be propagated by spores; it can only be propagated by division.

Overcollecting plants can sometimes cause the destruction of unique habitats and eventually the flora and fauna that inhabit these environments. That is why it is now legal to collect only seed in most countries. The *Franklinia alatamaha* and the *Metasequoia glyptostroboides* are two trees that were thought to be either extinct or nearly extinct in the wild; both are represented at Lakewold today. The franklinia, discovered in Georgia in 1765 by botanists John and William Bartram, cannot be found outside of cultivation. It is speculated that all the existing, cultivated trees descended from a few ancestors, or possibly even one tree from the Bartrams' collection. The dawn redwood, *Metasequoia glyptostroboides*, known as the "living fossil," was also thought to be extinct in the wild, but was discovered in China in the 1940s. Soon after, seeds were distributed to botanical gardens, parks, and individuals. Many of the old trees now growing in the United States originated from these seeds. Mrs. Wagner received her seedling from Professor Emanuel Fritz, Professor of Forestry at the University of California, Berkeley. Lakewold's metasequoia is a Washington State Champion, the tallest of its kind in the state.

Anyone who grows rare or unusual plants knows the fear that some event, pest, or culture error will result in the future loss of unique germoplasm, a risk that accentuates the importance of the distribution of such plants to institutions like Lakewold Gardens. In this way, species conservation not only demonstrates the importance of disseminating rare plants, it also exemplifies how the deep connections between people and plants tie together the rich history of horticulture.

OPPOSITE: TOP, LEFT TO RIGHT: Fewer than a dozen hardy terrestrial orchids of the Bletilla genus are available for Northwest gardeners. *Bletilla striata* blooms in late spring or early summer.

The little lily, *Erythronium tuolumnense* 'Pagoda', along with its various cousins, abounds in the wooded southeast section of the garden and along the circle drive. Because it blooms in late winter, few visitors enjoy the full benefit of these delicate heralds of spring.

Only ten species of the Ipheion genus are available. Lakewold's is *Ipheion uniflorum* 'Rolf Fiedler'. These small, bulbous perennials from South America are barely four inches tall, and bloom in late winter. They are useful along paths where they can be seen at short range and their honey-scented aroma can be enjoyed.

MIDDLE, LEFT TO RIGHT: The hardy *Cyclamen hederifolium* is another plant whose foliage holds as much interest as its flower. The heart-shaped leaves appear in mid-May, and are mottled with silvery green among their veins. By late summer the leaves are dormant, and the white, pink, or magenta flower, like a shooting star, appears in September. They produce cormlike tubers but are easily propagated from seed, which is sometimes dispersed by ants and slugs. They appear everywhere at Lakewold.

This little primrose from Japan, *Primula kisoana*, has a familiar looking blossom, but its hairy leaves set it apart from its relatives. It also refuses to remain where it has been planted, and prefers the gritty material of the footpath instead.

The common names for hellebores, Christmas rose or Lenten rose, attest to their late winter and early spring blooming season. The colors range from white through various shades of green to deep pink and purple. This *H. x hybridus* 'Heronswood Purple' blooms in February.

BOTTOM, LEFT TO RIGHT: 'Moonstone' is a hybrid of *R. campylocarpum* x *R. williamsianum*. Registered in 1933, it is an April-blooming, cream-colored variety listed as achieving three feet at ten years and about six feet in twenty years. *R. campylocarpum* is a species with light yellow flowers and was used in many early hybrids to get yellow flowers without much success. Usually the best hybrids were cream or a very light color. *R. williamsianum* usually produces the smaller, rounded leaves with reddish stems seen here. 'Moonstone' thus shows the best features of both its parents, and was a very common garden hybrid through the 1950s and '60s. It is still occasionally found in nurseries.

Native to the Himalayas, China, and Japan, this plant appears to be related to the more common witch hazel. However, the *Loropetalum chinense* 'Razzleberri' is one of only three species in the Loropetalum genus. Although marginally hardy in Lakewold's climate zone, this is a fully mature plant at five feet in height.

A western native, *Trillium rivale*, is a gem among native woodland wildflowers. At about seven inches tall, it is much smaller than the more familiar Western trillium (*T. ovatum*), whose common name is Wake robin, for its bright white flowers that appear in early spring (March and April) just when robin activity seems to wake up. *T. rivale* is found growing along streamside banks, giving it the name Brook wake-robin. It is geographically confined to the Klamath and Siskiyou mountains of Southwestern Oregon and California.

NOTE

1   Manuscript in the Wagner Home papers, p. 9.

chapter five

THE VISITOR EXPERIENCE
Vickie Haushild

or nearly half a century the private
gardens at Lakewold could be seen publicly only through images of the gardens
appearing in professional volumes—as in landscape architect Thomas Church's
own discourses, popular magazines like *Sunset* and *Architectural Digest*, and in
numerous feature articles in Northwest newspapers. All that changed in 1987,
when Mrs. Wagner donated the property to the nonprofit board Friends of
Lakewold, both to insure the preservation of the gardens and to open Lakewold
to the public. Only two years later small tours were available; today more than ten
thousand people visit the gardens annually.

Because it is so distinctly a private garden, docents routinely evoke the
continued presence of Mrs. Wagner by pointing out her color preferences and her
broad horticultural interests. The astonishing variety of historically important
plants that number into the thousands, thanks to her remarkable ability to sustain
Mediterranean plants in a Northwest wet climate—as with the santolina and
germander in the knot garden—are there for sharing, along with some of the
garden mistakes that inevitably come with experimentation, such as the small
bamboo groundcover that has proven almost impossible to eradicate.

For many visitors, the garden's ultimate charm lies in its scale. Its rooms are expansive, yet they do not dwarf the viewer, nor can they be seen from a single vantage point. Although both a strong axis and counter axis structure the formal garden area, the visitor is invited to meander about, to discover such rare plants of stature as the state champion trees, along with the numerous "hidden" treasures like the unimposing statuary, tiny scree gardens, Lilliputian mouse plants, the linearifolia rhododendrons, and the mature, but still small, Japanese maples whose lacy leaves are so finely cut they look a bit like spiderweb.

The nearly nine hundred rhododendrons and azaleas are visitor favorites, and their bloom period can span from January through June. The Himalayan blue poppy, *Meconopsis grandis*, has iconic status at Lakewold and thrives best in western Washington. In the water garden area, maples command such attention that it is impossible to keep labels attached. *Acer palmatum* 'Shindeshojo' with its bright-pink new leaves is perhaps the most photographed plant at Lakewold. It is flanked with the Full-Moon maple, *A. japonicum* 'Aconitifolium', whose lemon yellow early growth contrasts vividly with the pink of 'Shindeshojo' and the dark green of the native Douglas firs.

Gardens, of course, are not static, and well-designed gardens provide interests throughout the year. The importance of "bones" for a garden becomes clear in fall and winter, and the landscape architecture at Lakewold is actually more apparent when there are no blooms to distract the eye from the play of textures and forms.

Mrs. Wagner experimented and welcomed change, the current garden staff experiments and welcomes change, and the gardens continue to evolve. Flowering cherry trees, boxwood parterres, and dogwoods have been replaced with newer examples. Culinary herbs in the knot garden have given way to sedums and succulents. The formal parterres have been planted with a variety of summer-color material, and high-maintenance rose beds have been replaced by perennials. Yet even with these changes the strong sense of a personal, private, garden remains. Visitors speak of peace and tranquility, solitude, delight, and the appreciation of the pristine, elegant environment that is conveyed at Lakewold. Mrs. Wagner would have enjoyed those Edenic compliments. As she once observed, "It all began in a garden."

CLOCKWISE FROM TOP LEFT: The Lion fountain is located directly west of the swimming pool and is now almost completely obscured by the large rhododendrons that flank it. This view from inside the rhododendron forest gives us the best sense of his catlike qualities.

The *Acer griseum* (Paperbark maple) is a slow-growing, rather small tree whose most attractive feature is its peeling bark.

Although garden staff maintained the box edging for the parterres, Mrs. Wagner took it upon herself to keep the topiary birds in shape. This peacock occupied the terrace outside the sunroom.

Lakewold's *Acer palmatum* 'Shishigashira' (Lion's head maple) is unrecognizable as a maple until examined closely. Its short leaf stems and small, tightly clustered leaves give a mop-like appearance to the branches. One of the latest of the maples to turn color in autumn, its masses of yellow-gold leaves reinforce its common name, Lion's head.

LEFT: This Japanese maple, *Acer palmatum atropurpureum*, is located on the northwest sector of the circle drive. This bright pink color is its early spring foliage. Its summer color is quite close to that of the copper beach that stands behind it.

ABOVE: The Wagner grandchildren were often invited to bring their friends to spend the night. House staff with silver trays would provide lunches and picnics, the woods offered great hiding places, and the swimming pool was an ocean for toy boats when it wasn't in service for swimming.

ABOVE RIGHT: The original Carriage House, built in 1918, is now home to The Garden Shop at Lakewold. The English-style garden shop, located at Lakewold's entrance, has become a meeting place for local gardeners and out of town visitors. Docent-led tours of the gardens begin and end here.

While Lakewold is primarily a destination for gardeners, it has become more than a garden showplace. Over the past two decades, the yearly calendar shows a long list of events that have come about as clubs, nonprofits, businesses, and educational institutions have chosen to use both the house and the gardens for retreats, programs, and other activities. "Picnic and Pops" has filled the west lawn with hundreds of music lovers. Jazz concerts, too, have been popular. "Kids Day" has brought educational programs to a small army of future gardeners, and free tours for school groups are routine. Workshop space at Lakewold offers an off-campus environment for a wide variety of professional organizations, and each year limited numbers of free rental dates are made available to nonprofit charitable organizations. And of course the gardens provide limitless subject matter for drawing, watercolor, and photography classes from local junior colleges and universities. As shown by the growing numbers of those who bring their lunch to enjoy a quiet noon hour, or who visit Lakewold after work or with after-dinner guests in July and August, when the gardens are open on Wednesday evenings until eight p.m., all these occasions serve to stimulate interest in gardening and in garden spaces.

chapter SIX

PRESERVING LAKEWOLD'S INSPIRING LEGACY
Bill Noble

These photographs of Lakewold Gardens belie the fact that during World War II the Wagner family maintained the gardens with little help. Mrs. Wagner wrote: "My husband and son took turns cutting the lawn while I tended the boxwood parterres, transformed into a victory garden of fresh vegetables. Luckily, we engaged an elderly farmer and his wife, who cared for the cow we had acquired. Our cow was sheltered in the same box stall of the carriage house where 'Kitty' had stood. (My husband's uncle, Major Griggs, kept a number of thoroughbred horses.) . . . Son Cordy, at 13, attempting to set a record for speed in mowing the lawn, tripped and fell after eight straight hours of work, lost control of the lawnmower, and it went into the lake."

This book, a collaboration among gardeners, photographers, and historians who have been inspired by Lakewold, mirrors the nature of the very garden it chronicles. In this it parallels the garden itself, which reflects the grand sharing of sensibilities between Mrs. Wagner and the landscape architect Thomas Church, as well as between Mrs. Wagner and the skilled gardeners and horticulturists who worked together to make this into one of the most plant-rich and inspiring of Pacific Northwest gardens. Tall native conifers were brought together with many exotic and native plants to create a harmonious synthesis that encompasses both the serenity of the natural world and the cultivated universe of a garden. Stylistically the garden is also a conversation between classical and modernist styles, one created at a time when Pacific Northwest gardeners were searching for a new type of garden that would be at once livable and universal in its appeal and yet reflective of the special characteristics of the landscape that have come to define the region.

This tradition of collaboration is being taken a step further by the preservation of Lakewold beyond the lifetime of its makers. Mrs. Wagner left her garden to the public and invited The Friends of Lakewold to assume a role in

In early spring, this view of the
woods east of the walkway shows
how persuasively *Acer palmatum*
'Shindeshojo' appears as though it were
a tree in flower. Its mid-spring color,
here set off by sky-blue *Rhododendron
augustinii*, can be seen in illustrations at
pages 4 and 49.

keeping her original vision alive. Now, two decades on, a board of directors, staff, and volunteers are responsible for maintaining this vision and ensuring that the garden continues to touch the lives of its visitors and provide inspiration to a new generation of gardeners, designers, and plantspeople.

All the writers and photographers whose experience and vision appear in this book are gardeners whose lives have been enriched by their association with Mrs. Wagner and her keen plantsmanship. Their experience at Lakewold encourages the rest of us to make an effort to know the garden better as it moves through the seasons and the years. A garden remains vibrant as long as there are good gardeners tending it, and it cannot survive for long if it is not loved and cared for by the public for whom it was preserved. Gardens demand an audience. Visiting Lakewold, appreciating its beauty, and supporting the gardeners' work are all crucial to its preservation and continued development as a horticultural resource.

Mrs. Wagner's gift to the public is a legacy that is renewed each time a visitor experiences the excitement of chancing upon the much-coveted blue poppy in bloom, or observing the brilliance of a 'Ukon' cherry at the peak of its glory against the dark evergreen backdrop of native conifers. The garden offers up its peace and serenity to those of us in need of solace and respite and then captivates us with its magic as we get to know the trees, flowering shrubs, rhododendrons, and herbaceous plants that Mrs. Wagner sought out and so gracefully arranged. And herein lies the challenge of preserving personal gardens such as this. For how does a garden continue to take on a life of its own twenty years after its creator has left it behind?

Lakewold strives to maintain the serenity of a private refuge, and in the spirit of its creator must continue to move forward with new plants and perennial compositions that are constantly assessed and improved. Trees age and decline, pergolas collapse and are replaced, swimming pools require repair, and these expensive and necessary projects are required to preserve the structure and the feel of the garden. Venerable plants introduced by Mrs. Wagner call for knowledgeable gardeners with a sense of connoisseurship and the self-confidence to maintain what is time tested as well as to introduce new and unusual plants that surely would have been added by their original plant-obsessed owner. Preserving the big picture of the trees, structures, and the landscape design

ABOVE LEFT TO RIGHT: The sculptured relief carving of this plaque presents a curious menagerie of fauna. At the bottom, a gruff-looking lion appears, with a fluffy mane much like the one worn by Bert Lahr in *The Wizard of Oz*. Above him, in diagonal crossing formation, are an oversized hare, two long-legged birds, and a beaked and winged griffon. The rough, unfinished edges around the relief contrast with the high finish of the rest, suggesting that the work was never completed, or that the edges were originally hidden by a separate frame. The creator of this relief may well have been inspired by the upward diagonal patterning, with the feet-on-back, mouth-to-mouth biting characteristic of actual and fantastical creatures found in Romanesque art of Western Europe in the eleventh and twelfth centuries. It is uncertain whether the sculptor intended to match the specific symbolism used by his Romanesque forbears in his choice of the individual animals. In any case, in its present location the relief admirably expresses nature's upshooting vitality and competitiveness, where weeding and pruning are parts of the natural process.

Major Griggs was a collector of Asian art, and many of the Asian articles in the garden were brought here by him. About two feet high, this figure of a Shinto priest is probably from Japan.

This terra cotta figure, holding wheat sheaves in one arm, personifies summer in the form of the goddess Ceres; she probably held a harvesting tool, now lost, in her other hand.

ABOVE LEFT TO RIGHT: This elegant, eighteenth-century Chinese wallpaper greets guests in the foyer of the Wagner house.

The little Raphael angel fountain, about four and a half feet high, rests on the garage wall that serves as a southern terminus to the east terrace and the knot garden.

The Lakewold goddesses of Flora (spring) and Ceres (summer) have a male seasonal companion, this statue of Bacchus, god of wine and of the autumn season when grapes are harvested. He is easily identified by the relaxed fleshiness of a sybaritic life, the vine leaves in his hair, and the leopard skin over his arm, since leopards pulled his chariot and symbolize the wildness that strong drink can produce. Perhaps understandably, winter, the fourth season, commonly personified by a bearded Father Winter, is absent at Lakewold, a place that celebrates growth during every month of the year.

as a whole requires one set of skills, and the cultivation of woodland plants, alpines, and intricately woven knot gardens requires another. Expensive capital improvements and repairs are always just around the corner in a garden of this kind, and constant attention is demanded of those involved to stay on top of the garden as it develops, and to maintain and refine its intimate details.

To accomplish all these activities takes a team of gardeners and groundskeepers, as well as managers and boards of directors who must raise funds through memberships, annual appeals, special events, and admissions, and also administer a modest endowment. This is often difficult, and we have seen many important gardens disappear for lack of vision, funding, or successful management practices. Gardens at this level of personal expression are most threatened by the gradual decline in their owner's ability to maintain them and by the absence of an appropriate organization that can actively assume ownership and take on their supervision.

The Garden Conservancy was founded in 1989 to preserve exceptional American gardens for the education and enjoyment of the public. The Conservancy's guiding mission is to see that gardens such as Lakewold live and thrive beyond the lifetime of their founders and become important horticultural resources within their communities, and at the Conservancy we have worked with more than ninety gardens across the country that give voice to the regional and cultural expressions of a time and place and tell the stories of their individual creators.

In selecting gardens to work with, the Conservancy applies aesthetic, horticultural, and historical criteria. We are interested in gardens that demonstrate a creator's passionate engagement with the land, or that may illustrate the development of a particular garden style in a region, or stand as an outstanding integration with the natural or architectural environment. We believe diverse types and styles of gardens and innovative approaches to garden-making should be preserved. We look for gardens of outstanding horticultural merit that display unique collections of

A garden remains vibrant as long as there are good gardeners tending it, and it cannot survive for long if it is not loved and cared for by the public for whom it was preserved.

plants, diversity and variety of habitat, and a high quality of cultural conditions and maintenance. We help preserve gardens with special cultural or historical significance, whether regional or national, that may represent the style of the period in which they were developed or the influence of a noted designer or person of extraordinary ability. And in every case we examine the feasibility of the ability of a garden to last beyond the lifetime of its owner. We know we've succeeded when we match the next generation of talented gardeners with the exceptional gardens of today.

Documenting a garden is a critical part of helping its new managers understand the original design intent and how the garden might best continue to evolve. It is a pleasure to know that this book, with its historical overview of Lakewold's development, insights into the personalities of those most vital to it, and valuable plant lists, will go far in assisting all those who care for the garden to celebrate its fundamental achievements as well as the qualities that will carry its majestic beauty into the future.

Lakewold is one of the premiere estate gardens on the Pacific coast and host to thousands of guests and gardeners each year whose lives are touched in much the same way as with the authors of this book. We honor the creators—Mrs. Wagner and Thomas Church—and we treasure their legacy: Lakewold Gardens. Staff and volunteers maintain and preserve this living legacy for a fundamental reason: gardens have meaning—personal, historic, horticultural, aesthetic and spiritual. Each time we visit Lakewold, or any other garden, we have a new opportunity to contemplate, explore, and to reconsider the importance of our intimate relationship with the natural world.

LEGACY PLANTS

CHOICE RHODODENDRONS IN THE GARDEN

R. augustinii
R. azalea 'Rosebud'
R. 'Bambi'
R. barbatum
R. 'Bow Bells'
R. cinnabarinum ssp. *xanthocodon* var. *concatenans*
R. 'C.I.S.'
R. 'Dora Amateis'
R. erosum
R. 'Eulalie Wagner'
R. 'Eulalie Wagner' x *R. williamsianum*
R. forrestii
R. 'Fragrantissimum'
R. 'Grosclaude'
R. irroratum 'Spatter Paint"
R. 'King of Shrubs'
R. kiusianum
R. loderi 'King George'
R. luteum
R. 'Marinus Koster'
R. 'Muncaster Mist'
R. 'Nova Zembla'
R. oreodoxa
R. quinquefolium (Cork azalea)
R. 'Romany Chai'
R. rothschildii
R. 'Ruby Hart'
R. stenopetalum 'Linearifolium'
R. 'Thomwilliams Group'
R. wiltonii
R. yakushimanum var. 'Ken Janeck'

R. *irroratum* 'Spatter Paint'

R. 'Thomwilliams Group'

R. 'Ruby Hart'

R. *luteum*

R. *loderi* 'King George'

R. 'C.I.S.'

R. 'Grosclaude'

R. *cinnabarinum* ssp. *xanthocodon* var. concatenans

SIGNIFICANT SPECIMEN TREES AND SHRUBS

Acer circinatum 'Monroe'	Monroe's maple	Woodland area
Acer griseum	Paperbark maple	Woodland area
Acer palmatum 'Deshojo'	Japanese maple	Woodland area
Acer palmatum 'Shishigashira'	Lion's head maple	Picnic area
Actinidia kolomikta	Arctic kiwi	Garage and sunroom
Betula utilis 'Jacquemontii'	Jacquemont's birch	Woodland area
Carpinus betulus	European hornbeam	Woodland area
Cornus controversa 'Variegata'	Giant dogwood	Lookout area
Cornus kousa	Kousa dogwood	Helen Weyerhaeuser Tea Room (gazebo)
Cornus kousa 'Chinensis'	Kousa dogwood	Swimming pool area
Cornus mas	Cornelian cherry	Gazebo
Cornus nuttalii	Pacific dogwood	Woodland area
Cryptomeria japonica 'Spiralis'	Japanese cedar	Woodland area
Cunninghamia lanceolata	China fir	Woodland area
Davidia involucrata	Dove tree	Woodland area
Edgeworthia papyrifera	Paper bush	Wagner house
Embothrium coccineum	Chilean flame tree	Woodland area
Enkianthus campanulatus	Furin-Tsutsuji	Circle drive
Euonymus planipes	Spindle tree	Woodland area
Fagus sylvatica 'Atropurpurea'	Copper beech	East lawn
Franklinia alatamaha	Franklinia	Circle drive
Hamamelis virginiana	Virginia witch hazel	Rose garden
Magnolia sieboldii	Seibold's magnolia	East lawn
Magnolia x *soulangiana*	Saucer magnolia	Shade garden
Paulownia tomentosa	Empress tree	West lawn
Pieris japonica	Lily of the valley bush	Circle drive
Prunus serrulata 'Shirotae'	Mt. Fuji cherry	Brick walk
Prunus serrulata 'Ukon'	Ukon cherry	East lawn
Pseudotsuga menziesii	Douglas fir, wolf tree	East lawn
Styrax japonicum	Japanese snowbell	Automobile court
Styrax obassia	Fragrant snowbell	Shade garden

Magnolia sieboldii

A. palmatum dissectum 'Goshiki Shidare'

Cornus controversa 'Variegata'

LAKEWOLD AND GARDENS FOR PEACE

In 1998, the Lookout element of Lakewold was placed on the list of Gardens for Peace, an International Network of Gardens to Promote Peace. To date the list of gardens includes:

1988 Swan Woods Trail, Atlanta, Georgia
1989 Tbilisi Gardens, Tbilisi, Republic of Georgia
1991 Royal Botanical Garden, Madrid, Spain
1993 Agnes Scott College, Decatur, Georgia
1998 Lakewold Gardens, Tacoma, Washington
1999 Pastoral Institute, Nairobi, Kenya
2000 Oakhurst Community Gardens, Decatur, Georgia
2000 Columbia Theological Seminary, Decatur, Georgia
2001 Caroline C. Black Garden, New London, Connecticut

2002 Sarah P. Duke Gardens, Durham, North Carolina
2002 Sadako Peace Garden, Montecito, California
2002 State Botanical Garden of Georgia, Athens, Georgia
2003 Chandor Gardens, Weatherford, Texas
2003 Cheyenne Botanical Gardens, Cheyenne, Wyoming
2003 Charlottesville Historical Society Garden, Charlottesville, Virginia
2004 The Serenity Garden, Atlanta, Georgia

– Source: gardensforpeace.org

STATE CHAMPION TREES

A champion tree is the largest known example of its kind, representing the maximum growth of a species. The Washington State Big Tree Program has registered over a thousand trees belonging to more than eight hundred species and cultivated varieties that are the largest in the state. This very important program recognizes, documents, and helps preserve these majestic examples of biological maturity.

– Source: Robert Van Pelt, *Champion Trees of Washington State*
(Seattle: University of Washington Press, 1996).

Prunus serrulata 'Tai Haku'

Acer palmatum atropupureum	Red Japanese maple	Circle drive
Acer palmatum	Japanese maple	Woodland area
Halesia caroliniana var. *monticola*	Mountain silver bell	Circle drive
Ilex crenata 'Meriesii'	Japanese holly	Woodland area
Ilex x *altaclerensis* 'Camelliifolia'	Camellia-leaved highclere	Circle drive
Metasequoia glyptostroboides	Dawn redwood	East lawn
Parrotia persica	Persian ironwood	Woodland area
Prunus lusitanica	Portuguese laurel	Wagner house
Prunus serrulata 'Tai Haku'	Tai Haku cherry	Wagner house
Prunus subhirtella 'Pandora'	Pandora cherry	Woodland area

Meconopsis grandis

SIGNATURE PERENNIALS, BULBS, AND EPHEMERALS

Arisarum proboscideum	Mouse plant	Tom Gillies Hardy Fern Garden
Cyclamen hederifolium	Neopolitan cyclamen	Circle drive
Danea racemosa	Alexandrian laurel	Shade garden
Erythronium hendersonii	Henderson's fawn lily	Circle drive
Erythronium oregonum	Oregon fawn lily	Woodland area
Erythronium revolutum	Mahogany fawn lily	Woodland area
Galanthus nivalis	Snowdrop	Rock garden / Large scree
Gentiana aucaulis	Gentian	Rock garden / Large scree
Helleborus niger	Christmas rose	Shade garden
Helleborus orientalis	Lenten rose	Shade garden
Hepatica nobilis	Liver leaf	Tom Gillies Hardy Fern Garden/ Shade Garden
Meconopsis grandis	Himalayan blue poppy	Varying locations
Sanguinaria canadensis	Bloodroot	Tom Gillies Hardy Fern Garden
Vancouveria planipetala	Inside-out flower	Tom Gillies Hardy Fern Garden

Cyclamen hederifolium

Helleborus argutifolius

Italicized page numbers
indicate illustrations.

PHOTOGRAPHY CREDITS

A note on dating of the photographs: Charles Pearson, 1962; Dick Busher, 1981–1984; Corydon Wagner III, 1980–1990; Judy Wagner, 1990–2010; Ronald Fields, 2010. All others are contemporary.

Susan Allen, back cover flap, bottom; Katie Burki, 21 (bottom row right), 97 (middle row left), 113 (third from top); Dick Busher, inside front cover, 1, 2–3, 6, 16 (right), 33 (right), 35, 39–42, 44, 48–49, 50–53, 55, 60–63, 65, 67, 83, 85, 90, 98, 104–105, 118–119, back cover; Katherine Easton, back cover flap, second from top; Ronald Fields, 21 (top row right, bottom row left), 25 (bottom row right), 36, 38 (right), 74 (center), 93, 94, 95 (bottom), 97 (top row middle and right, center row middle and right, bottom row left, center, right), 101 (top row right), 102, 106, 108 (center), 109, 112 (center), 113 (top); John Furlong, back cover flap, fifth from top; Robert L. Jones, back cover flap, top; Charles Pearson, 46–47, 82 (top), 87; Nicholas Nyland, 108 (left); Lyle Peniston, 120; Irene Russo, 25 (left), 112 (bottom); Gail Stickley, 74 (right); Jeffrey Sturges, front cover, 117; *Sunset* magazine, back cover flap fourth from top; Mike Swale, back cover flap, seventh from top; Marc Treib, 81, 82 (bottom), 84, 88 (top); Corydon Wagner III, 4–5, 10–11, 15, 17, 21 (top row left), 22–24, 32, 33 (left), 34 (center and right), 37, 56–59, 69, 72, 76, 97 (top), 101 (bottom row right), 107 (right), 108 (right), 110, 112 (top); Judy Wagner, 16 (left), 25 (top right), 34 (left), 38 (left), 45, 64, 71, 74 (left), 75, 89, 91, 95, 101 (top row left, bottom row left), 103, 107 (left and center), 113 (second from top, bottom); John Wilcox, 111 (all images), back cover flap third from top; Brian Williams, back cover flap, sixth from top.

SPECIAL THANKS

Special thanks for the following friends who in countless ways contributed to the completion of this book: Alison Andrews, Steve Balint, Gary Becker, Dale Bobb, Mrs. Joseph Carman, II, Joe Carman III, Wendy Dunnan, Hannah Fields, Zaixin Hong, Wendy Isenhart, Barbara Lindburg, Adelade Mueller, Nicholas Nyland, Martha Robbins, Irene Russo, Gail Stickley, Anne Traver, Elodie Vandevert, Cordy Wagner IV, Wallace Weston, Wendy Weyerhaueser, and the entire staff of Lakewold Gardens.

VISITING LAKEWOLD GARDENS

Lakewold Gardens is located at 12317 Gravelly Lake Dr SW, Lakewood, just south of Tacoma, Washington, and is open to visitors year-round. 253.584.4106 www.lakewoldgardens.org

Lakewold: A Magnificent Northwest Garden

© 2011 The Jardin Group

Printed and bound in China by Artron Color Printing

Ronald Fields, editor
Judy Wagner, producer

Contributing authors: Dan Hinkley, Valerie Easton, Ronald Fields, Steve Lorton, Marc Treib, Katie Burki, Vickie Haushild, Bill Noble

Creative director: Anne Traver
Design: Nancy Kinnear
Color management: Dick Busher
Text editing and proofreading: Sigrid Asmus

Published by The Jardin Group
P. O. Box 39780
Lakewood, Washington 98406

www.lakewoldgardens.org

Distributed by University of Washington Press
P. O. Box 5096, Seattle, WA 98145 U.S.A.
www.washington.edu/uwpress

ISBN 978-0-295-99108-5
Library of Congress Control Number: 2010939263

Permissions: pp. 8, 70 photographs from the Wagner family papers are reproduced by permission of the Wagner family; pp. 27, 28, 30, and 31, photographs from the Joseph Carman III family papers, are reproduced by permission of the Carman family. Photographs by Charles Pearson at pp. 46–47 (C626-7) and 82 (top, C626-8) are reproduced by permission of the University of Washington Libraries, Special Collections. Photographs at pages 78 and 80 are reproduced by permission of Thomas Church Collection, Environmental Design Archives, University of California, Berkeley.

Map by Scott Bailey

The paper used in this publication meets the minimum requirements of American National Standard for Information Sciences—Permanence of Paper for Printed Library Materials, ANSI Z39.48-1984.

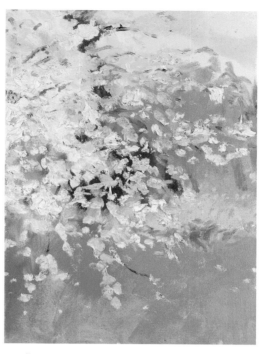

Merrill Wagner
May #5
2004
Oil on canvas
14 x 10 in.
Collection of the artist
Photo: Jeffrey Sturges

These plaques on Lakewold's terrace
are constant reminders that the seasons
order the patterns of life in a garden.
They are also timeless analogies of the
divisions of life—infancy, youth, maturity,
and old age—celebrated in literature
and in the visual arts. Each new year is
a opportunity for regeneration and joy
in the abundance of a garden.